A New Life For Bud

By Linda Vital

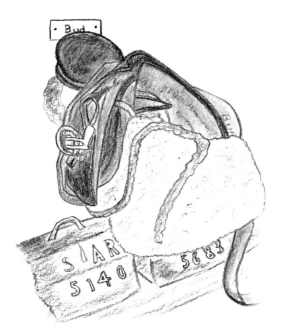

Copyright © 2009
by Lynda Vital.
35438-VITA

Library of Congress Control Number: 2007901111

ISBN: Softcover 978-1-4257-5297-2
Hardcover 978-1-4257-5298-9

This is a work of fiction. Names, characters,
places and incidents either are the product of the
author's imagination or are used fictitiously, and any
resemblance to any actual persons, living or dead,
events, or locales is entirely coincidental. This book
was printed in the United States of America.

Book Designer: Nicolo Manreal

To order additional copies of this book, contact:
Xlibris Corporation
1-888-795-4274
www.Xlibris.com
Orders@Xlibris.com

HORSEFEATHERS CENTER
1181 Riverwoods Rd
Lake Forest, Il 60045
Phone: (847) 234-2411
info@horsefeatherscenter.org
OR
Linda Vital at (847) 732-7819

Inquiries and donations are welcome!

DEDICATION

to Bratlee and Cavalier...
inseparable friends and perfect gentlemen
(most of the time!)

CHAPTER ONE

It was Bud's favorite day of the whole year – March 17, the day of the St Patrick's Day Parade in the city of Chicago, and it was a beautiful, sunny day!

Bud was a police horse, and every day he worked very hard. Each day he woke up early, ate some hay and oats, and waited for his friend, Sergeant Ray McNair to come. Sgt.McNair groomed him, saddled him up, and then said,"OK, Bud, time to go out on patrol!" Sgt McNair was always happy to see Bud, and Bud was always happy to go to work. He never knew what excitement lay ahead!

Most days were pretty routine. People respected policemen on horseback, so there usually wasn't much trouble to attend to. Sometimes there would be a big event going on in the city and Bud would be sent in to do some crowd control, which was always a challenge. One day a year , Bud would march in the St Patrick's Day parade, and it was the highlight of his year. There were lots of people, lots of music and noise, and best of all, lots of children!

Bud wasn't able to see many children on the beat, as they were usually in school during the day. However, lots of children came out to see the St.Patrick's Day Parade, and Bud just loved children.

When he was a young colt, out in the pasture with his Mom, he remembered a boy who used to come to see him. The boy would bring lots of treats for Bud- apples and carrots and peppermints. So he thought the world of children.

As was the custom on this day of days-Sgt McNair came early and groomed Bud, and got his coat extra nice and shiny. "You have to look perfect today, Bud!" he exclaimed. "This is a special St Pat's day Parade for you, as it's your twentieth anniversary!" Yes, this was Bud's twentieth year of being a police horse, and the twentieth time he would march in the parade. .

Sgt. McNair led Bud out with the other officers and their horses;it was time to get into formation for the march. Bud was the oldest horse there, and he was proud to be in the lead. He couldn't wait to hear the crowds cheering, and see the children gather around him, hugging him and giving him lots of treats. Life was good!

The fire engine blared its siren, the bag-pipers started playing ,and the parade began. The policemen on horseback followed the pipers, threading their way through the crowded streets.

Every once in awhile, the parade would stop while a band played a song. When that happened, kids from the crowd came out to see the horses. This was a special treat for Bud. He loved their soft voices and he loved how some of them would scratch him under his chin. During one of these stops, while the horses were being showered with attention, Bud noticed something interesting, something rather strange.

There was a boy up ahead on the sidewalk who did not come out to see the horses – he just sat there. Bud wondered why, and then noticed that the boy was sitting in a chair with wheels. Bud had seen these chairs before, but didn't quite understand them, being a horse and all. The boy looked kind of sad. Bud wanted to walk over and see him, but all of a sudden, the music stopped and he had to start marching again.

As he walked by ,Bud nickered a little at the boy as a way of saying "Howdy." Bud hoped the boy understood. He must have, because a big smile appeared on his face; this made Bud feel really great. The rest of the parade went well, and Bud enjoyed it thoroughly, but his mind kept going back to that boy.

CHAPTER TWO

Danny thanked his Mom and Dad for taking him to the parade. They knew it was a big treat for him. "My favorite part was seeing the police horses!" he said. "I would so love to learn how to ride one of those guys some day!" Danny's Mom and Dad just looked at each other.....they knew that would never happen. Danny was confined to a wheelchair, after all. How could he ever do anything physical, let alone ride a horse?" His Dad smiled at him and said,"Maybe someday , Danny, you never know!

Danny was twelve years old, in the seventh grade, and he had never been able to walk. Most of the time he accepted this, because his Mom and Dad took him to cool places, and he had several hobbies. He liked to draw and play video games, of course.However, it was hard to make friends , as most guys his age were into sports and stuff like that.

Plus, some of the girls were getting really cute, but none seemed too interested in him at all. After all, he'd never exactly be able to dance with any of them! So he was lonely at times.

Sometimes when he was by himself in his room, he would cry and wonder why the doctors couldn't fix his legs. Other times he would imagine jumping out of bed, running downstairs, hopping on a bicycle, and speeding down the street to school. He knew it would never happen, but it didn't hurt to pretend.

CHAPTER THREE

After the parade, all the horses returned to their stalls for a much-needed rest. Bud was tired after the parade, but so happy. He had gulped down many treats, and had many pats and hugs, from many happy children. All the policemen were in the stable now-Sgt McNair and his good buddies, and they were all talking about the parade. "Bud was great today, Ray!" said one of the officers. "He sure was!" said Sgt McNair. "Not bad for an old guy!"

Bud was happy to hear the praise, but did not quite understand what Sgt. McNair meant by "an old guy."

"It will be strange next year without Bud leading the way," said another officer. Sgt McNair said he'd rather not think about that right now. Bud was very surprised and confused by what he had heard. What did Officer Abram mean, "without Bud?" "Where am I going?" thought Bud. He thought and thought, but just couldn't figure it out, so he decided that maybe he had misunderstood, being a horse and all.

So he started thinking about the parade again, and all the fun, but also about the boy in the wheelchair . He thought again about how happy he was that he had made that boy smile.

CHAPTER FOUR

Danny wasn't doing too well in his math class. He didn't particularly like his teacher, and he didn't understand fractions at all. He was really frustrated. His Mom noticed how sad he seemed to be a lot of the time, and one night as he was going to bed , she asked him if anything was wrong.

"I don't know," he said."I haven't felt right since the St Patrick's Day Parade, actually. It was so much fun, but I wanted to go up and pat the horses,and I couldn't because I'm stuck in this stinkin' wheelchair." Danny's Mom felt so bad. It was hard for her to see her son suffer. He wanted to be like the other kids, right? He wasn't a baby any more- he was twelve years old-almost a teen-ager, and he wanted to be a big guy.

"I wish I could ride one of those beautiful police horses, but hey-that isn't ever going to happen , is it," he said.

"Don't lose hope, Danny," said his Mom. People with disabilities can learn to do all kinds of things. You've seen the wheelchair marathoners, haven't you? There are more and more new ideas coming out to help kids like you. Who knows-maybe some day you COULD learn to ride a horse!"

CHAPTER FIVE

Bud was feeling a little weird. Sgt McNair and some of the other officers were in the tack-room, and Bud overheard them talking...about him!

"Gosh, Ray, what will you do after Bud retires? You'll really miss him!" asked one of the men.
Ray didn't even want to think about it. He just couldn't imagine it...he had been partnered with Bud for 20 years! "I know Bud has been slowing down a bit- a touch of arthritis, perhaps. He has so much heart-he's a great worker, not to mention my best buddy. He really isn't ready to be put out to pasture."

"Put out to pasture? Who-me?" thought Bud. He'd heard a little about that. That's what happens when a horse can no longer do his job, or when his owner can't keep him any longer or ...doesn't want him any more. Well, none of those things apply to me! I love my job and I love Sgt McNair and he loves me." Nevertheless, Bud couldn't help being a little worried.

CHAPTER SIX

One day, Danny was sitting in the cafeteria next to a table of boys who were on the basketball team. They were talking about practice or something like that. Danny was sitting with some of his own friends, so he wasn't paying much attention. However, his ears perked up when one of the guys mentioned his little sister. "She's disabled and has to go to her horse therapy class this afternoon. Can I have a ride to practice?" That was the only part of the conversation Danny was really interested in. He wondered what kind of class the little girl went to. He didn't know these boys, as they didn't have much in common, and he was pretty shy. However, as the day went on, he was so curious, he decided he would work up the courage to ask the boy about the class.

The next day , he had a chance to talk to the boy, who was standing in the hallway reading notes on the bulletin boards. Danny nervously cleared his throat, took a breath and wheeled himself up to the boy. He hoped the boy wouldn't be mad at him for listening in on his conversation!

"Excuse me," said Danny. He introduced himself to the boy, who told him his name was Kevin. "I don't mean to butt into your business, but I was in the cafeteria the other day and I heard you say something about your little sister going to horse-riding class or something."

Kevin was instantly friendly, much to Danny's relief. "Yeah, she is disabled and goes to a stable and takes riding lessons. She really likes it. She can actually steer the horse all by herself!"

"Wow!" exclaimed Danny. "Is it very far away?"

Kevin told him it was only about four miles away, out in the woodsy part of town. He said his sister had been riding since she was five years old, and there were lots of other kids with all kinds of challenges who went there. He told him all about the horses, and that there were ponies and police horses in the program.

This was exciting news to Danny."Police horses?"he said. "Boy, I wish I could sign up!"
Kevin said that his Mom could call Danny's Mom and tell her all about it. Danny couldn't believe it. He had been brave, had made a friend and found out about a place where maybe-just maybe-he could have his dream come true!

CHAPTER SEVEN

Sgt McNair was given the word from the Chief. Bud would have to retire at the end of the summer. He felt so bad, but he knew it was for the best. Bud deserved a rest. But what would happen to him? Where would he go? Sgt. McNair was determined to find a good new life for Bud, the horse who had helped him faithfully day in and day out, without complaint.

One night, he came home from work to find his wife in front of the TV set . She called him over excitedly. "Quick, there's a good show on here about horses!" she exclaimed. Ray walked over and stood in front of the TV.

The narrator talked about something called "therapeutic riding." They showed an arena where disabled people were riding horses. Some were small children with autism. Riding the horse and performing fun tasks, like hitting a ball hanging from the ceiling, helped them focus and concentrate. Other riders had problems with their muscles. The movement of the horse helped make their muscles stronger. Some of the horses were ponies and some were large horses-horses like Bud. One of the leaders of the riding program said that calm, well-trained horses were needed for the job. He even mentioned that police horses were the best candidates, as they had had rigorous training in handling difficult situations.

Ray was really excited. "I'm going to look around and see if there are any of these therapeutic riding places around here. That would be a perfect job for Bud!" he said.

CHAPTER EIGHT

Well, Danny's Mom talked to Kevin's Mom, who told her all about "Happy Trails", the riding stable where Kevin's sister had her lessons. Danny's Mom called right away, and got Danny an appointment for an evaluation at noon on the following Saturday. He was very excited about it, and also a little nervous, but Kevin told him not to worry.

"They're really nice there. They try to match you with a horse that is suited to your needs. You can probably ride a big horse. You play games and do exercises on the horse. It's fun, but it's also work. It will make you stronger."

Danny showed up at noon and he and his Mom met with a man named Dave Wilson,the director of the therapeutic riding program. He explained to them how riding a horse could help Danny's muscles get stronger. He talked to them about horses, and Danny met the horses that worked there. Dave explained some basic rules about riding to Danny. He told him that when you ride a horse, you should sit tall, look straight ahead, and most of all, trust your horse and yourself.

Finally, Dave put a helmet on Danny and said, "Let's ride!" Danny couldn't believe this was happening to him. He remembered the big horse he had seen at the St Pat's Day Parade and how much he had wished he could ride him. And now his wish was almost coming true.

A pretty, white Arabian horse was led out into the arena by a boy named Mark. "This pretty gal's name is Pearl, Danny," said Mark. "I will be her leader, and you will have Dave to instruct you and there will be a side-walker right next to you during your lesson."

Dave helped Danny out of his wheelchair and up to the mounting blocks. Danny could walk a little, with assistance, and he had special braces on his legs to help strengthen them. "Just lean over Pearl, put your hands on her mane, and your left foot in the stirrup, Dan," said Dave. "We'll help you swing your other leg over the saddle."

Danny did just as he was told, and before he knew it, there he was....sitting on top of a horse! It was like magic! The next half-hour was, as Danny described it to everyone later, the most fun he had ever had in his life. "I felt like I was sitting up on top of the world up on that horse, "he exclaimed. "My wheelchair no longer existed. I felt like the the horse's legs were my own!"

CHAPTER NINE

Sgt. McNair was not in a hurry to go to work. Today was the day they were to move Bud over to "Happy Trails". The Chief had been totally agreeable to donating Bud to the therapeutic riding program. Ray was happy about that, and he had tried to enjoy every day with Bud till the time would come for them to part. That day was today.

As Ray groomed Bud for the last time, he worked really slowly and talked to him gently.
"Well, Bud, this is going to be harder for me than it is for you. I don't know what I'm going to do without you. But I'm happy about one thing. We found the best new job in the world for you. It's nice and close, and I can visit you any time I want. "

"What does he mean….new job?" thought Bud." I don't need a new job-I love this job! Is my pal going to send me away for some reason?" Bud was really confused.

As if reading Bud's mind, Ray went on to say, "You know, there comes a time when we all have to slow down-that goes for humans and horses,too. You've done a great job, but we can't let you do this work any more. You have to retire. Don't worry, I'll have to retire someday, too! But we found you a great new job, and guess what-you're going to get to work with children!"

Bud perked up a little when he heard that, remembering how much kids like to give horses treats. "Well, maybe that's not such a bad idea," he thought.

Satisfied that he had made Bud look as handsome as he could be, Ray led his partner and friend out of the stable.

As Bud passed his old friends, he thought of how he would miss them. His best buddy nickered at him as he went by, as if to say,"Good luck, Bud! Don't forget us!"

Ray brought Bud out to the trailer. Bud entered slowly, not knowing what lay ahead, but totally trusting in his friend.

CHAPTER TEN

Delivering Bud to "Happy Trails" was the hardest thing Sgt McNair had ever done in his life. However, Bud was blessed by the fact that he was, after all, a horse, and horses are amazingly curious animals. Coming out of the trailer and seeing a totally new environment was just thrilling for him! He followed Ray down the aisle and they found his new stall, which Ray inspected thoroughly.

It had to be good enough for his best friend. He saw that there was plenty of nice bedding and lots of room for Bud to lie down and roll around. There were nice, clean water buckets, and the stall had a dutch door so he could look out and see all the action.

It was a busy place, with lots of workers bustling around-grooming horses, saddling horses for lessons, and giving out treats. Just the sight of the treats made Bud's mouth start to water.

"Gosh, I wouldn't mind having a treat right now!" thought Bud. Just at that moment, a few of the teen-age workers spied Bud.

"Say, there's the new horse the police department is donating!" said one of the girls. All of a sudden, there was a big commotion. Everyone got excited when the program got a new horse. They all wanted to come get to know him. So, suddenly Bud was surrounded by people. Sgt McNair stepped aside so Bud could be patted and fussed over. He knew right then that everything would be all right. Sgt McNair gave Bud a hug and told him he'd come visit tomorrow. Although he had to brush a tear from his eye, he left with a big smile on his face.

CHAPTER ELEVEN

Bud was so busy being fussed over, he didn't even notice that Sgt McNair had gone. The day went so fast. There were so many new things going on, he didn't have time to think about the stable, his old job, or anything else.

First, a couple of kids came in and groomed him. Well, he had always enjoyed that, but he had never had kids do it before, just police officers. So it was a new joy, especially because once in awhile, one of the kids would present him with a carrot or an apple.

"Hey Bud, we have to bring you into the arena now and show you around," Mark said. Mark led Bud out of his stall and into a big , bright arena. It was a little strange, as big rubber balls were hanging from the ceiling, and buckets of bean-bags and various board games were hanging on the walls.

"We have to help you get used to the place before you start your new job, Bud," said Mark. "You see, there will be children riding you who will hit the balls and play the games, and we want to be sure you can stand nice and still and not be nervous."

"Piece of cake!" thought Bud. "After all, I AM a police horse! "

They led Bud around and hit the balls hard and threw the bean-bags and made all kinds of noise, and Bud was perfect. Next, they had a few people ride him. He liked that a lot. He trotted and cantered around and around the arena,obeying all the commands he was given.

"I like riding around in circles like this-it sure is different than walking the beat with Sgt McNair," thought Bud.

"Bud, you did great! We'll tell the instructors you're ready for action!" said Mark.

Thinking about his pal, Sgt McNair, suddenly made Bud sad. He stood in his stall that night and remembered all the good times they had had together. He wondered what Sgt McNair would do the next morning when he woke up and realized he had no horse to groom and ride. Since he was a horse, Bud was not inclined to brood about the past, and immediately cheered up by thinking about what a great day he had had. He knew Sgt McNair would be all right, and would probably visit him tomorrow.

CHAPTER TWELVE

Sure enough, when Sgt McNair woke up in the morning, he just lay in bed for a minute He wasn't excited at all about getting up. What on earth would he do when he got to the station and there was no Bud waiting for him? He had dreaded this day. However, he carried on. He had some new duties, just like Bud did, and he performed them well and headed out at the end of the day. Of course, he couldn't wait to get to the stable to visit Bud, as he had promised.

He showed up just as Bud was being tacked up for one of his lessons. Ray was pleased to see that the people who worked with Bud were treating him kindly. Bud looked very content in his new home. Ray sat in the bleachers surrounding the arena and watched as his partner carried a small rider on his back. The child was only about five years old, but he knew how to use the reins and everything.

"Turn your horse to the right," said the instructor. The child gave a little pull on the right rein, and Bud instantly did what he was asked. The little boy went around the arena and over the ground poles and played some games. Bud was amazed that such a small child could be such a good rider. Sgt McNair was so proud! How quickly his horse had taken to his new life. Although Ray missed him terribly, he was so glad to see how well Bud was doing.

CHAPTER THIRTEEN

After only a few weeks on the job, Bud had become one of the favorite and most trusted of all the horses. He was loved by humans and horses alike. Pretty Pearl, the white Arabian, particularly liked him! He was really enjoying his life at "Happy Trails" and didn't think too much about his old job at all. However, he did love seeing his pal, Sgt McNair, when he came to visit.

Just as he thought his life couldn't get any better, one day a wonderful thing happened. He was out in the arena, ready and waiting for his next lesson,when a boy in a wheelchair arrived at the stable. The boy looked awfully familiar to Bud.

"Hi, Danny, how was your vacation?" Dave asked the boy. "We have a new horse for you to try today."

Danny said he had had a great time on his trip, but he couldn't wait for his lesson. "I really missed riding," he said. "Is that my new horse?" For some reason, he felt like he had seen this horse before.

"This new guy's name is Bud. He started here while you were gone. He's a retired police horse," said Dave.

"I knew it! I knew I recognized him!" exclaimed Danny. "This is the horse I saw at the parade last year. I was so sad that day, and this horse made me smile. He's the whole reason I wanted to learn how to ride. I can't believe he's standing right here in front of me." Danny shook his head in disbelief.

At that moment, Bud also recognized Danny. He was overjoyed. He was also a little amazed at how different Danny looked now. The sad boy that had haunted his memory looked much stronger now, more confident in himself.

And boy, could he ride! Dave decided that Danny and Bud were perfect for each other. From then on, the two rode together every Friday afternoon. They became fast friends.

CHAPTER FOURTEEN

As time went on, Sgt McNair often showed up to watch Danny's lesson with Bud. He often took pictures of them riding. He showed the pictures to all Bud's old friends at the police station. Everyone missed him there, but they were very excited about his new life."

One day, Ray showed up at the stable with a big smile on his face. He watched Danny and Bud have their lesson and came up to see them afterwards.

"Hey, old pal, how're you doing?" he asked. "Danny-nice riding!" He had a pocketful of peppermints for Bud. Bud knew just what pocket they were in;horses have good memories. He nickered with appreciation.

"Say, Dan, I have a surprise for you. The St Patrick's Day Parade is a few weeks away, and we were talking about how much we were going to miss not having Bud around to march in it this year. Well, the Chief of Police had an idea, and he talked to the Mayor of the city about it. He thought that maybe Bud could march after all, with a group of workers from "Happy Trails." It would call attention to the program here, and it would be fun for us all.

Danny thought that was a great idea. "I'd be so happy to see Bud march in the parade again," he said.

Sgt. Mcnair laughed and said,"You don't quite understand, Danny. We were hoping you would agree to ride Bud in the parade yourself!"

CHAPTER FIFTEEN

It was March 17th already, time for the parade. "Boy, a lot has happened in just one year," thought Danny. He quickly got dressed and gobbled up his breakfast as fast as he could. He had never been so excited! His folks dropped him off at the stable and headed downtown so they could get a good spot on the parade route.

Everyone at Happy Trails bustled around, getting ready for the big event. . Mark and Dave had groomed Bud and the two other horses that would be marching, and then the horses were carefully loaded into a trailer. Danny and the other people who would be marching with the horses got into a van, and they all headed for the parade grounds.

When the marchers and horses reached the parade grounds, they quickly got into formation. Some of the kids carried a big banner and some carried balloons. The horses wore special banners. Dave helped Danny mount Bud, and he and the other two horses and their riders brought up the rear.

Bud's heart leaped when the siren of the police car started the parade. He could not believe he was here again, this time with a whole new group of friends. He saw all the police officers and his old buddies, and he nickered to them all happily. They were all proud of him as he rode by with Danny on his back.

As the parade turned the corner, Danny saw his family waving, and he smiled and waved back. He also saw some of the guys from his class, including Kevin, who had helped him find "Happy Trails." All the guys yelled loudly when they saw him. "Way to go, Danny!" they called.

After the parade, as the marchers began to scatter and return home, Sgt McNair managed to find Bud and Danny. "Bud, I'm so proud of you. I missed you so much after you left. I was so worried about what would happen to you. But I can see that you are happy in your new life. I hope you can keep up the good work for a long, long time."

Bud looked at his old partner and wished he could thank him with all his heart for finding such a wonderful new place for him. But, being a horse, all he could do was give him the biggest neigh he could manage, and nudge him in his favorite pocket, and gratefully accept a treat!

THE MOUNTED POLICE
written by Sandy Synnestvedt Ruch

Although Bud and Sgt. McNair are fictional, they are drawn from the real life experiences of the Chicago mounted police unit.

Chicago police used horses in the early 1900s and through World War II. In the 1940s, with the mechanical advancement of cars and motorcycles, "modernization" replaced the police horse, and the mounted unit was disbanded.

In 1974, an effort to have more of a police presence in Grant Park in Chicago resulted in the pilot program of today's mounted police unit. It was patterned after the National Parks mounted police training in Washington, DC. Chicago began its pilot with just ten police horses, and the number doubled by the following year. By 1977 they had 24 horses. The current number of 30 stands at the optimum number they can house and maintain.

The Chicago Police Department stables its 30 police horses at the old South Shore Country Club – now South Shore Cultural Center. The stable, at 7059 S. South Shore Drive, is over 100 years old. The mounted unit is an important part of Chicago's law enforcement today.

"Bud" in our story, was a gelding, a neutered male. This is a requirement for police horses. For police work, a horse must be dark: bay, like Bud, who is a rich brown with black mane and tail; chestnut, a reddish brown; or black. The dark color is required so that the horses present a uniform appearance, and one horse won't visually stand out from the others. At medium height, 15.3 hands, (a hand is four inches, measured at the withers) Bud meets the minimum height requirement for police horses, at least 15.2 hands.

Bud was six years old when he began his work with the police. Most police horses start at about age five, although occasionally as young as three or four. Bud had been donated to the police, and his former owner requested that they keep his name Bud. If not for this request, he would have been given a new name, that of a police officer who was killed in the line of duty.

While some police horses are donated, others are purchased from a reputable dealer who knows exactly what the requirements are for the mounted police unit. More than any physical characteristic, the quality that sets a police horse apart is his disposition. He must be steady, brave, calm, patient, resilient, and dependable. Bud was all of this, and he thrived on the work. Bud's career with the mounted police lasted for over 15 years.

As "Sgt. McNair" learned, it is not easy to become a mounted police officer. Sgt. McNair was one of 15 applicants selected for his training class, out of the city's police force of over 13,000. He had to be a three-year veteran of the police force before he could even apply. The training to become a member of the mounted police unit is rigorous, to ensure not just technical excellence, but also that successful graduates are those who really want to ride a police horse. Even before Sgt. McNair began training, he knew that, out of the 15 who start a class, only six are likely to make the grade.

In the 12-week course, Sgt. McNair learned every aspect of horsemanship from the ground up: mucking stalls, grooming and caring for his horse, tacking up, riding to strictest standards, and crowd control. For the first six weeks training was inside. Field work began in the seventh week, with training maneuvers in city parks and on the lakefront. Each day, Sgt. McNair rode a different horse until, in the twelfth week, matching up horse and rider began. Bud and Sgt. McNair made an ideal pair, completed the training together, and began their fifteen-year partnership.

Each morning when he got to the stable, Sgt. McNair would groom Bud, then tack up and load Bud into the trailer. Next he'd go upstairs for roll call and the day's assignment. After that, it was time to go out to start the day. For each eight-hour shift, Bud and the sergeant would be on patrol for about six hours. In the summer, much of their duty was patrolling parks. In the winter, they patrolled mostly downtown. Sgt. McNair and Bud, and half the unit, had the morning shift, starting at 8:30, while the afternoon shift began at 3:30.

Occasionally, like when the President comes to the city, the entire unit is called to report for that special duty. During any event that attracts crowds, the unit makes its presence known, because mounted officers are so visible from the ground. When a crowd actually needs to be moved, e.g., after the big St. Patrick's day parade when it is time for all the revelers to go home, the mounted police line up side by side and "sweep" the street, and the crowd disperses. When necessary, even one mounted officer can clear a wide space, just by "turning his horse on the forehand," so that the hind end swings in a wide arc, from which pedestrians back off!

Working crowd control, or riding routine patrols, the mounted police are a very powerful, memorable, and positive presence in the city. Bud portrays one special role of many police horses everyday – he's a goodwill ambassador!

Special thanks to the Chicago Police Department and especially to Officer John Schaffer, head trainer of the mounted police unit, for his help with background information and tour of the stable.

Horses and Healing
written by Sandy Synnestvedt Ruch

Since antiquity, the horse and human bond has been known for its healing power. Use of the horse in a therapeutic role, from helping wounded veterans regain functionality, to augmenting the development of struggling children, has grown dramatically since the mid-twentieth century. Two principal programs have developed, which may appear similar from a distance, but have different focus:

Hippotherapy, i.e., treatment with help of the horse (from the Greek "hippo" meaning horse) is conducted by specially trained physical, occupational, and speech therapists who use the rhythmic, multi-dimensional motion of the horse as a treatment tool. Aided by a horse handler, the therapist directs the movement of the horse to influence the "rider", who may be positioned in various ways on the horse. The front-to-back, side-to-side movement of the horse closely simulates the movement that a person's body experiences in walking, and can have a powerful effect on individuals who have a movement dysfunction.

Therapeutic riding is taught by registered instructors who have been certified by NARHA, the North American Riding for the Handicapped Association. In this program, riders learn to control the horse and develop as much independence as they are able. In contrast to "hippo," here the rider is learning horsemanship – and still benefiting from the movement and energy of the horse. Whatever support the riders need, whether leading the horse or walking alongside to stabilize their position in the saddle, is provided by specially trained volunteers.

The program for each rider is customized to the specific objectives tailored to his/her ability. Second only to emphasis on safety is a large dose of fun - stretching, reaching, throwing, laughing all help the rider to relax, engage, and improve. Sessions may include games – throwing bean bags, shooting baskets, "red light green light," Simon Says - to develop coordination, focus attention, and interject fun, as appropriate for the individual's needs, maturity, and functionality.

In the hippotherapy and therapeutic riding programs, we see individuals with a wide range of disabilities, including

1   Physical Disabilities
2   Cognitive Disabilities
3   Behavioral Challenges
4   Emotional Challenges
5   Attention Disorders
6   Autism Spectrum Disorders

Benefits that riders experience may include:

1   Increased muscle strength and tone
2   Increased balance and mobility
3   Increased range of motion
4   Improved confidence and self esteem
5   Greater ability to focus and stay on task
6   Behavioral improvements
7   Increased problem solving ability

Although physical and developmental benefits are numerous, there are intangible, even sweeter, benefits as well. Picture a wheelchair-bound child, accustomed to looking up at the world, being able to see the world from atop a horse, even learning how to direct this large animal; it is hugely empowering, and leaves the rider feeling "on top of the world."

With a therapy horse's non-judgmental approach and quiet trust, riders are motivated to learn and grow to their full potential. Whether for a small child with Downs Syndrome, a teenager with Cerebral Palsy, an adult with Multiple Sclerosis, or an older stroke victim, each little accomplishment is a victory, and the experience is positive, productive, and often exuberant.

There can be big or little breakthroughs at every turn, healing and strengthening on many levels. A child who was non-verbal to begin with, becomes joyfully talkative over time. Some children who could not hold themselves upright in the saddle when they began hippotherapy grow strong enough to "graduate" to therapeutic riding. Seeing a person's newly developed ability overshadow their disability – what a gift!

For more information on hippotherapy, visit the website of the American Hippotherapy Association: www.americanhippotherapyassociation.org.
For more information on therapeutic riding, go to the website for NARHA, www.narha.org

Biography
Sandra Synnestvedt Ruch

Over the past six years, I've been on a healing path – quite literally walking it every day – either leading or walking beside the horses who work their magic in a therapeutic program for riders with special needs.

My first contact with therapeutic riding was as an intern working toward an Equine Science degree. Even before that, I'd sensed a connection between horses and healing, but I didn't quite know how that connection worked – or whether it was real or imagined.

In that internship, my mentor shared this quote with me:

The bravest and the strongest are the kindest and the gentlest to the neediest.

Finally, I now see the connection: a big, retired police horse being ever-so-gentle with our frailest rider; our biggest and boldest helpers being always kind to the unsure or vulnerable; and reciprocally, we humans taking care of our dedicated equine partners, most tenderly when they become frail.

I dedicate my work to the bravest and the kindest, Cavalier.

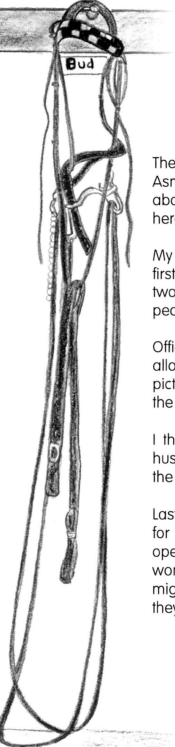

ACKNOWLEDGEMENTS

The first person I would like to thank is my fellow - volunteer, Cheryl Asmar, who said one day that "someone here should write a book" about our program. I just couldn't get the idea out of my head , so here's the result.

My two dear friends, Nancy Dickie and Sandy Ruch, proof-read my first draft and helped me to polish my words. Sandy also wrote the two appendices for me. I felt that I would like this book to educate people about the horses and about programs like ours.

Officer John Schaffer, of Chicago's Mounted Police Unit, very kindly allowed me to visit him and the horses at their headquarters. The pictures I took there were used extensively in the drawings of Bud in the first part of the book.

I thank my family for supporting me in my project, especially my husband, Walter, who had enough faith in me to pay for the publishing!

Last, but most importantly, I will be forever grateful to Nick Coyne for teaching me to ride (he had the patience of a saint!), and for opening up a whole new world to me. Working with the horses is too wonderful to describe. I only hope that this book, my gift to them, might make people more fully appreciate them and the important job they do.

Edwards Brothers, Inc.
Thorofare, NJ USA
February 27, 2012